EXPLORING SPACE

Astronauts

by Colleen Sexton

Consultant:
Duane Quam, M.S. Physics
Chair, Minnesota State
Academic Science Standards
Writing Committee

BLASTOFF! READERS

3

BELLWETHER MEDIA · MINNEAPOLIS, MN

Note to Librarians, Teachers, and Parents:

Blastoff! Readers are carefully developed by literacy experts and combine standards-based content with developmentally appropriate text.

Level 1 provides the most support through repetition of high-frequency words, light text, predictable sentence patterns, and strong visual support.

Level 2 offers early readers a bit more challenge through varied simple sentences, increased text load, and less repetition of high-frequency words.

Level 3 advances early-fluent readers toward fluency through increased text and concept load, less reliance on visuals, longer sentences, and more literary language.

Level 4 builds reading stamina by providing more text per page, increased use of punctuation, greater variation in sentence patterns, and increasingly challenging vocabulary.

Level 5 encourages children to move from "learning to read" to "reading to learn" by providing even more text, varied writing styles, and less familiar topics.

Whichever book is right for your reader, Blastoff! Readers are the perfect books to build confidence and encourage a love of reading that will last a lifetime!

This edition first published in 2010 by Bellwether Media, Inc.

No part of this publication may be reproduced in whole or in part without written permission of the publisher. For information regarding permission, write to Bellwether Media, Inc., Attention: Permissions Department, 5357 Penn Avenue South, Minneapolis, MN 55419.

Library of Congress Cataloging-in-Publication Data

Sexton, Colleen.
Astronauts / by Colleen Sexton.
  p. cm. – (Blastoff! readers. Exploring space)
  Summary: "Introductory text and full-color images explore what astronauts do in space. Intended for students in kindergarten through third grade"–Provided by publisher.
  Includes bibliographical references and index.
  ISBN 978-1-60014-284-0 (hardcover : alk. paper)
  1. Astronauts–Juvenile literature. I. Title.
TL793.S4137 2010
629.45–dc22   2009037957

Text copyright © 2010 by Bellwether Media, Inc.
Printed in the United States of America, North Mankato, MN.
010110   1149

Contents

Astronauts are people who fly **space shuttles** or work in space. The word *astronaut* means "star sailor."

People who become astronauts work in many different jobs. Some are in the military. Some are scientists, **engineers**, doctors, or teachers.

There are different kinds of astronauts. Some astronauts are pilots. They fly space shuttles.

Pilots can also be **commanders**. A commander is in charge of a space shuttle and makes sure everyone aboard is safe.

Some astronauts are **mission specialists**. They make sure the space shuttle systems work correctly.

Payload specialists are also members of space shuttle crews. They are not trained as astronauts. Their job is to work on experiments.

Astronauts train at the Johnson Space Center in Texas. They take science classes and study how space shuttles work. They often practice using tools and machines

Sometimes they train underwater to feel like they are in space.

Astronauts learn how to survive a crash landing on Earth. They practice using **parachutes** and swimming in **flight suits**.

Astronauts train for about three years. Then they are ready to blast off into space!

There is little **gravity** in space.
Astronauts are weightless.
They float from place to place
inside the shuttle.

Astronauts strap themselves onto special beds or into sleeping bags to sleep.

Astronauts must be careful when they eat. Their food can float away!

Astronauts have a **mission** every time they travel to space. They sometimes bring supplies to a **space station** where other astronauts live and work.

Astronauts may bring a **satellite** in the space shuttle. The pilot uses a robot arm to put the satellite into **orbit**.

Mission specialists might
make a **space walk** to fix
part of a space station.
They wear special suits.

The astronauts are ready to go home. The pilot fires the engines and steers the space shuttle back to Earth.

The astronauts shut
down the space
shuttle controls. They
are ready to leave
the space shuttle.
Mission completed!

Glossary

commanders—astronaut pilots who are in charge of space missions

engineers—people who plan and build machines

flight suits—the orange jumpsuits that astronauts wear during the space shuttle's launch and return to Earth

gravity—the force that pulls objects toward each other; gravity keeps objects from moving away into space.

mission—a special job or task

mission specialists—astronauts who help the commander oversee all work during a mission; mission specialists make sure the shuttle systems are working correctly.

orbit—the path that an object takes when it circles the sun or a planet

parachutes—large pieces of lightweight material with ropes; people use parachutes to float to the ground after jumping from an aircraft.

payload specialists—people who are part of a space shuttle crew and do scientific experiments

satellite—an object that is sent into space to orbit Earth; satellites can help predict weather, take pictures of Earth, or beam TV signals to Earth.

space shuttles—spacecraft that carry astronauts into space

space station—a laboratory in space

space walk—to leave a spacecraft and move around in space; astronauts wear space suits when they make a space walk.

To Learn More

AT THE LIBRARY

Harrison, James. *Astronaut for a Day*. New York, N.Y.: DK Publishing, 2005.

McCarthy, Meghan. *Astronaut Handbook*. New York, N.Y.: Alfred A. Knopf, 2008.

Todd, Traci N. *A Is for Astronaut*. San Francisco, Calif.: Chronicle Books, 2006.

ON THE WEB

Learning more about astronauts is as easy as 1, 2, 3.

1. Go to www.factsurfer.com.

2. Enter "astronauts" into the search box.

3. Click the "Surf" button and you will see a list of related Web sites.

With factsurfer.com, finding more information is just a click away.

BLASTOFF! JIMMY CHALLENGE

Blastoff! Jimmy is hidden somewhere in this book. Can you find him? If you need help, you can find a hint at the bottom of page 24.

Index

The images in this book are reproduced through the courtesy of: NASA, front cover, pp. 4-5, 4 (small), 6, 7, 8, 9, 10 (small), 10-11, 12, 14, 15, 16 (small), 16-17, 18 (small), 18-19, 20-21, 20 (small); NASA / Science Photo Library, p. 13.

Blastoff! Jimmy Challenge (from page 23).
Hint: Go to page 17 and suit up.

2/15